Dumb Jokes for Adults

Steve Burt

BURT CREATIONS

Dumb Jokes for Adults
Steve Burt

BURT CREATIONS

ISBN 979-8-9877213-5-3

Copyright 2025 by Steven E. Burt

All rights reserved

Cover: BookCoverZone Stiletto 21970

Contact information:

Steven E. Burt

17101 SE 94th Berrien Court

The Villages, FL 32162

352 391-8293

"You don't stop laughing when you grow old, you grow old when you stop laughing."
— George Bernard Shaw

Dedication

To all of those adults who came past my ***Dumb Jokes for Kids*** book tables at all those arts and crafts shows over the last ten years and wisecracked, "How about some Dumb Jokes for Adults?" Well, here they are, including the risqué and a few politically incorrect. Enjoy.

About the Author

Steve Burt is the award-winning author of the ***Dumb Jokes for Kids*** series, the ***Recipe for Adventure*** chapter books for 6-12 year-olds, the Maine ***Allagash Gargouilles*** adult thrillers, the ***FreeKs*** psychic teen mysteries, three collections of inspirational stories, and eight weird tales collections that include a 2004 Bram Stoker Award winner.

His books have won the New York Book Festival grand prize, the Florida Book Festival grand prize, a dozen New England Book Festival awards, and five Mom's Choice Awards gold medals.

Steve and his wife Jolyn split their year between Wells, Maine and The Villages, Florida.

DUMB JOKES FOR ADULTS

At my age rolling out of bed is easy.
Getting off the floor is a whole other story.

A man finds his seat at the Super Bowl, but notices that there's an empty seat between him and the next guy. "Who in their right mind would miss the Super Bowl?"

The man next to him smiles and says, "Well, actually this was my wife's seat. She passed away recently, and we had already purchased the tickets."

The first guy says, "Oh, I'm sorry for your loss," but then thinks for a second and adds, "Don't you think it would have been nice to take one of her family members to the game?"

The man looks ahead and replies, "I would have, but they are all at her funeral right now.

*It turns out that when asked who your favorite child is, you're supposed to pick one of your own. I know that now.

Woman: "While out walking along the edge of a pond just outside my house in The Villages with my soon-to-be ex-husband, discussing property settlement and other divorce issues, we were surprised by a 12-foot alligator which suddenly emerged from the murky water and began charging us with its large jaws

wide open. She must have been protecting her nest because she was extremely aggressive. If I had not had my little Beretta .25 caliber pistol with me, I would not be here today!"

Man: "You shot a gator with a small-caliber pistol? That must have been one heck of a shot."

Woman: "No, not the alligator. My estranged husband's knee cap. The gator got him easily, and I was able to escape at a brisk walk. I saved a fortune in lawyer fees, and his life insurance was a really big bonus!"

Man in bed with his wife …
Slides his hand slowly across her shoulders … across
her waist … under her neck …under her back … and
suddenly stops.

Wife (in a romantic voice): Why
did you stop?

Man: Got the remote. You go back to sleep.

Two guys decide to go ice fishing.
They set up their gear, cut a hole in the ice, and start
fishing.
Suddenly, a voice booms
from above: "There are
no fish under the ice."
They look around, but
they don't see anyone.
They move to another spot, cut a hole, and try again.
The voice says, "There are no fish under the ice."
Spooked, they look around again.
One of them nervously asks, "Is that you, God?"
The voice replies, "No, it's the ice rink manager."

A drunk man who smelled of beer sat down on a subway seat next to a priest. The man's tie was stained, his face was smeared with red lipstick, and a half-empty bottle of gin was sticking out of his coat pocket. He opened his newspaper and began reading.

After a few minutes, the man turned to the priest and asked, "Say, Father, what causes arthritis?"

"Mister," the priest said, "it's caused by loose living, being with cheap, wicked women, too much alcohol, and a contempt for your fellow man."

"Well, I'll be damned," the drunk man muttered, returning to his paper.

The priest, thinking about what he'd said and his harsh tone, nudged the man and apologized. "Sorry, I didn't mean to come on so strong. How long have you had arthritis?"

"Oh, I don't have it, Father," the man answered. "I was just reading here that the Pope does."

A lady goes to the bar on a cruise ship and orders a Scotch with two drops of water. As the bartender gives her the drink she says, "I'm on this cruise to celebrate my 80th birthday and it's today.

The bartender says, "Well, since it's your birthday, I'll buy you a drink. In fact, this one is on me."

As the woman finishes her drink, the woman to her right says, "I would like to buy you a drink, too."

The birthday girl says, "Thank you. bartender. I want another Scotch with two drops of water."

"Coming up," says the bartender.

As she finishes that drink, the man to her left says, "I would like to buy you one, too."

The woman says, "Thank you, bartender. I want another Scotch with two drops of water." 

"Coming right up," the bartender says. As he gives her the drink, he says, "Ma'am, I'm dying of curiosity, why the Scotch with only two drops of water?"

The 80-year-old woman replies, "Sonny, when you're my age, you've learned how to hold your liquor. Holding your water, however, is a whole other issue."

My spouse and I have reached the difficult decision that we do not want children. If anybody does, just send us your contact details and we can drop them off tomorrow.

Saw a storefront sign that read, "We treat you like family." Yup, not going there.

In a recent password audit, someone was found to be using the following password MickeyMinniePluto HueyLouieDeweyDonaldGoofySacramento. When asked why such a long password, she said she was told that it had to be at least 8 characters long and include at least one capital.

With old age comes wisdom … and early-bird specials!

A city slicker moved to the country and bought a piece of land. He went to the local feed and livestock store and talked to the proprietor about how he was going to take up chicken farming. He then asked to buy 100 chicks.

"That's a lot of chicks," commented the proprietor.

"I mean business," the city slicker replied. A week later he was back for another 100 chicks.

"Boy, you are serious about this chicken farming," said the store owner.

"Yes, if I can iron out a few problems."

"Problems?" asked the proprietor.

"Yeah," said the city slicker. "I think I planted the last batch too close to each other."

Muldoon lived alone in the Irish countryside except for a pet dog he had for a long time. The dog finally died and Muldoon went to the parish priest.

"Father," he said. "My dog is dead. Could you possibly be saying a Mass for the poor creature?"

The priest said, "No, we can't have services for an animal in the church. But there's a new denomination down the road apiece. No telling what they believe, so maybe they'll do something for the animal."

Muldoon said, "I'll go right now. By the way, do you think $50,000 is enough to donate for the service?"

Father: "Why didn't you say the dog was Catholic?"

Patient: "Oh Doctor, I'm starting to forget things."

Doctor: "Since when have you had this condition?"

Patient: "What condition?"

During my check-up I asked the Doctor, "Do you think I'll live a long and healthy life then?"
He replied, "I doubt it somehow. Mercury is in Uranus right now."
I said, "I don't go in for any of that astrology nonsense."
He replied, "Neither do I. My thermometer just broke."

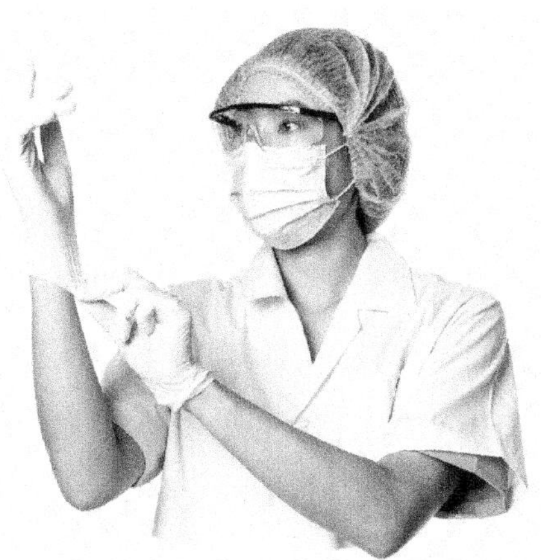

*I'm getting older and wider instead of older and wiser!

Double standards. Burn a body at a crematorium, you're being "respectful." Do it at home and you're "destroying evidence."

I can't believe I forgot to go to the gym today. That's seven years in a row now.

At the service, the pastor asked about answered prayers. A lady rose and said, "I do. A month ago my husband Jim had a terrible bike wreck. His scrotum was crushed. The pain was awful. Doctors didn't know if they could help him." The congregation's men gasped audibly as they imagined Jim's pain.

"Jim was unable to hold me or the children because of the pain. We prayed as the doctors performed a delicate operation. They pieced together the crushed remnants of Jim's scrotum and wrapped wire around it to hold it in place." More men squirming.

She continued, "Now, Jim is out of the hospital. The doctors say, with time, his scrotum should recover completely." All the men sighed with relief.

The pastor rose and asked if anyone else had anything to say.

A man stood up and walked slowly to the podium. He said, "Hi, I'm Jim, and I would like to tell my wife, the word is *sternum*."

Ad posted outside an accounting firm: "HELP WANTED. Must be able to type 70 words per minute. Computer literacy required. Must be bilingual. EQUAL OPPORTUNITY EMPLOYER."

A dog walked into the accounting office and applied. The employer took one look at the dog, shook his head and said "I can't hire a dog." The dog pointed at the words EQUAL OPPORTUNITY EMPLOYER.

The employer said, "OK, type this letter." The dog typed it without a mistake at 70 words a minute. 

The employer then said, "Then can you put these figures into spreadsheet, make a program to feed it into the mainframe, process it in the General Ledger Module and give me the Balance Sheets and Profit and Loss Statement?" The dog did all of that.

The employer shook his head, pointed at the ad, and asked, "But are you bilingual?"

The dog replied, "Meow!"

A farmer is showing off his new invention to his friends: a pig with a wooden leg.

"Why does the pig have a wooden leg?" a man asks.

"This pig is special, the farmer says. "My house caught fire. The pig dragged me out, saved my life!"

"Amazing! But why does he have a wooden leg?"

The farmer continues, "Another time, my son fell in the river. The pig pulled him out. Saved him, too!"

"Incredible! But why the wooden leg?"

The farmer finally says, "Well, when you have a pig that special, you don't eat him all at once."

* Billion-dollar idea. A smoke detector that shuts off when you yell, "I'm just cooking!"

"Momma," asked Susie, "why do you always cut the ends off of the sausages before you put them in the pan?"

"Oh, that's just the way my mother always did it," the mother explained. "You'll have to ask her."

The next time her grandmother visited, Susie asked, "Grammy, why do you and Momma cut the ends off of the sausages before you put them in the pan?"

"Oh, that's just the way my mother always did it," says Susie's grammy. "You'll have to ask her."

So when the family visited Susie's slightly senile great-grandmother at the nursing home, Susie asked, "Why do you and Granny and Mummy always cut the ends off the sausages before you put them in the pan?"

"Oh, my Lord," says Great Grammy. "Are they still using that stupid little frying pan?"

*When I say "the other day" I could be referring to any time between yesterday and fifteen years ago.

An elderly Irish lady visits her physician to ask his advice on reviving her husband's libido. When he suggests Viagra, she says, "Not a chance. He won't even take an aspirin."

Doc says, "How about Irish Viagra? It's Viagra dissolved in his morning cup of coffee. He won't even taste it. Let me know how it goes."
She called the doctor the very next afternoon.

"How did it go?" he asked.

"Oh faith, bejaysus and begorrah, doctor, it was terrible. Just horrid, I tell ya! I'm beside meself!"

"Oh, no! What in the world happened?"

"Well, I put the Viagra in his morning coffee, and he drank it. It took effect almost immediately, and he jumped straight up out of his chair with a smile on his face, a twinkle in his eye, and his pants a-bulging. Then, with one fierce swoop of his arm, he sent the cups, saucers, and everything else that was on the table flying, ripped me clothes to tatters and passionately took me there, right on top of the table. Twas a nightmare, I tell ya, an absolute nightmare!"

"A nightmare?" doc asks. "Wasn't the sex good?"

"Why sure, best sex I've had in 25 years, but doc, I'll never be able to show me face in Starbucks again!"

At my age, the only pole dancing I do is while holding on to the safety bar in the bathtub.

The biggest lie I tell myself is, "I don't need to write that down; I'll remember it."

I spend a lot of time holding the refrigerator door open looking for answers.

Two engineers were standing at the base of a flagpole, looking at its top. A woman walked by and asked what they were doing.

"We're supposed to find the height of this flagpole," said the first engineer, "but we don't have a ladder."

The woman took a wrench from her purse, loosened a couple of bolts, and laid the pole down on the ground. Then she took a tape measure from her pocketbook, took a measurement, and announced, "Twenty-one feet, six inches," and walked away.

The second engineer shook his head and laughed, "A lot of good that does us. We ask for the height and she gives us the length!"

*My kids laugh because they think I'm crazy. I laugh because they don't know it's hereditary.

A plane takes off from Newark Airport and a blonde in Coach gets up and sits down in First Class. The flight attendant checks her ticket and tells the blonde she paid for Coach and must sit there.

The blonde says, "I'm blonde, I'm beautiful, I'm going to Toronto, and I'm staying here."

The attendant goes and tells the pilot and co-pilot about her, so the co-pilot goes to the blonde and explains she paid for Coach and must return there.

The blonde repeats, "I'm blonde, I'm beautiful, I'm going to Toronto, and I'm staying here."

The co-pilot tells the pilot, who says, "Let me handle this." He goes to the blonde and whispers something. She says, "Oh," and returns to her seat in Coach.

The amazed flight attendant and co-pilot ask the pilot what he said to get the woman to move so easily.

"I told her First Class doesn't go to Toronto."

A Russian truck driver stops at a traffic backup. He sees a policeman walking down the line of stopped cars to briefly talk to the drivers. As the policeman approaches the truck, the truck driver rolls down his window and asks, "What's going on?"

Policeman: "A terrorist is holding Putin hostage in a car. He's demanding 10 million rubles, or he'll douse Putin in petrol and set him on fire. So we're asking drivers for donations."

Driver: "Oh, ok. How much do people donate, on average?"

Policeman: "About a gallon."

A wife got so mad at her husband she packed his bags and told him to get out. At the door she yelled, "I hope you die a long, slow, painful death."
He turned and said, "So, you're saying you want me to stay?"

A 90-year old man was being interviewed on the secret to long life. The cameras rolled as he explained that his secret was to never drink or chase loose women. The back bedroom door opened and a barely dressed young woman ran out to grab an ice tray.

From the back room came, "Woman, get back here!"

 She answered, "Coming, big boy," then nodded at the cameras and disappeared back into the bedroom.

"Who is that?" asked the reporter.

"That's Dad," said the old man. "Drunk, as usual."

A retired man volunteers to entertain patients in assisted living homes and hospitals. He visited one hospital in Brooklyn and brought along his portable keyboard. After telling jokes and singing songs at  patients' bedsides, he bade them farewell and said, "I hope you get better."

One elderly gentleman replied, "I hope you get better, too."

A backwoods family took a vacation to New York City. One day, the father took his son into a large building. They were amazed by everything, especially the elevator at one end of the lobby. The boy asked, "What's that, Pa?"

The father responded, "Son, I ain't never seen anything like this in my life. I don't know what it is!"

While the boy and his father were watching in wide-eyed astonishment, an old lady walked up to the moving walls and  pressed a button. The walls opened and the lady walked between them into a small room. The walls closed and the boy and his father watched small circles of lights above the walls light up. They continued to watch the circles light up in the reverse direction. The walls opened again, and a voluptuous 24-four-year old woman stepped out.

The father turned to his son and said, "Boy, go get your ma!"

Three friends stranded on a deserted island find a magic lamp. The genie agrees to grant each a wish.

"I want to go home," says the first friend. The genie grants her wish.

"Me, too," says the second. The genie sends him home.

"I'm lonely," says the third friend. "I sure wish my friends were back here."

Two crows were in a field when they noticed a figure that looked like a man in the distance.

"See over there? What is that?" asks the first crow.

The second crow takes a long look, "That's a scarecrow. Looks authentic, doesn't it."

"How can you tell it's a scarecrow and not a person?" asks the first crow.

"Look at its hand," the second says. "No cellphone."

Elon Musk, the Pope, and a hippie were on a plane that developed engine trouble. The pilot stepped from the cockpit, announced they were going down, and grabbed a parachute and jumped. Which left two parachutes for three passengers.

Elon Musk announced, "I'm the modern world's greatest visionary—electric cars, space travel, and more. I clearly have to live." He grabbed one of the two parachutes and bailed out.

The Pope said to the hippie, "My son, I've lived a long, full life. You're young and have your whole life ahead of you. Take the last parachute. Live in peace."

"Don't worry," the hippie answered. "There are actually still two parachutes."

"How so?" the Pope asked.

"Well," the hippie said. "The world's greatest visionary just took my backpack."

I swerved my Harley to avoid hitting a deer, lost control and landed in a ditch. I crawled up to the road and flagged down a new convertible driven by a beautiful woman who asked if I was okay. "I think so," I said, leaning on the car door.

"Get in," she said. "I'll take you to my place so I can clean and bandage that nasty scrape on your head."

"That's nice of you," I answered, "But I don't think my wife will like me doing that!"

"I'm a nurse," she insisted. "I need to see if you have other injuries." She was very pretty and very persuasive, so I agreed, but repeated, "I'm sure my wife won't like this."

At her place, after a couple of cold beers and the bandaging, I said, "I feel a lot better, but I know my wife is going to be really upset so I'd better go now."

Don't be silly!" she said, smiling. "Stay for a while. She won't know anything. By the way, where is she?"

"My guess," I said, "is that she's still in the ditch."

A man's nagging wife died suddenly on a trip to Jerusalem.

Funeral director: "Sir, it would cost about $45,000 if we send her home back to the States. It'd only be $500 if we bury her here in Jerusalem."

Man: "Ship her home."

Funeral director: "But sir, why don't you bury her here in the Holy Land and save a lot of money?"

Man: "A long time ago a man was buried here and three days later he rose from the dead. I can't take that chance."

Wife asks her husband: "How many women have you ever slept with?"

Husband responds: "One, two, three, four, you, five, six… six total."

A Texan walks into a pub in Ireland. He says, "I hear you Irish are a bunch of hard drinkers. I'll give $500 American dollars to anybody in here who  can drink 10 pints of Guinness back-to-back."

The room is quiet, and no one takes up the Texan's offer. One man even leaves.

Thirty minutes later the same gentleman who left shows back up and taps the elderly Texan on the shoulder. "Is your bet still good?" asks the Irishman.

The Texan says yes and asks the barkeep to line up 10 pints of Guinness. Immediately the Irishman tears into all 10 of the pint glasses, drinking them all back-to-back.

The other pub patrons cheer as the Texan sits in amazement. The Texan gives the Irishman the $500 and says, "If y'all don't mind me askin', where did you go for that 30 minutes you were gone?"

The Irishman replies, "Oh, well, first I had to go to the pub down the street to see if I could do it."

A cruise ship passes by a remote island, and all the passengers see a bearded man running around and waving his arms wildly. "Captain," a passenger asks, "who is that man over there?"

"I have no idea," the captain says, "but he goes nuts every year when we pass him."

At a wedding the pastor asked if anyone had anything to say about the union, as it was their time to speak or forever hold their peace.

The moment of silence was broken by a young woman carrying a child. She started walking toward the pastor. Everything quickly turned to chaos.

The bride slapped the groom. The groom's mother fainted. The groomsmen shot each other looks, not sure how to save things. The pastor asked the woman, "Can you tell us why you came forward?"

The woman replied, "We can't hear at the back."

A blind man enters a bar and finds his way to a barstool. After ordering a drink and sitting there for a while, the blind guy yells to the bartender, "Hey, you wanna hear a politically incorrect blonde joke?"

The bar goes quiet. In a husky voice the woman next to him says, "Before you tell that joke, you should know something. The bartender is blonde, the bouncer is blonde and I'm a 6-foot-tall, 200-pound blonde with a black belt in karate. The fella sitting next to me is blonde and he's a weightlifter. The woman to your right is a blonde and a pro wrestler. Think about it, mister. You still wanna tell that blonde joke?"

The blind guy says, "Nah, not if I'm gonna have to explain it five times."

*My girlfriend and I are trying this whole "long-distance relationship" thing. I have to stay 100 feet away from her at all times. Also, the police say I should stop referring to her as my girlfriend.

A husband and wife are shopping in their local supermarket. The husband picks up a case of beer and puts it in their cart.

"What do you think you're doing?" asks the wife.

"They're on sale, only $20 for 24 cans," he replies.

"We can't afford 'em. Put 'em back," she orders.

They carry on shopping. A few aisles farther on, the woman picks up a $40 jar of face cream and puts it in the basket.

"What do you think you're doing?" asks the husband.

"It's my face cream. It makes me look beautiful," replies the wife.

Her husband retorts, "So does 24 cans of beer, and it's half the price."

That's him, lying there in Aisle 5.

A man is shipwrecked on a small island. After a few days he runs into natives who have just lost their chieftain. Their high priest tells the man he is the first outsider in 20 years. If he passes three tests, they accept him as their new chief. The man agrees.

The priest shows him a clearing with three straw huts. "In the first hut, you'll find 20 gallons of our native beer. You must drink all of it. In the second hut is a gorilla with a sore tooth. You must pull his tooth and survive to pass that test. In the third hut is the ex-chieftain's daughter. You must make love to her until she can take no more."

The man agrees and three hours later walks unsteadily out of the first hut and goes toward the second hut. The priest asks if he would like to have a rest, but the man declines and staggers into the hut. After two hours he comes out covered head to toe in blood and scratches. Still drunk, he turns to the priest.

"Now lead me to that girl with the sore tooth."

A pastor's wife was expecting a baby, so he stood before the congregation and asked for a raise. After much discussion, they passed a rule that whenever the pastor's family expanded; so would his paycheck.

After 6 children, this started to get expensive and the congregation decided to hold another meeting to discuss the pastor's expanding salary. 

A great deal of bickering ensued as to how much the pastor's additional children were costing the church, and how much more it could potentially cost.

After listening for about an hour, the pastor rose from his chair and spoke, "Children are a gift from God, and we will take as many gifts as He gives us."

Silence fell over the congregation until a little old lady stood and said, "Rain is also a gift from God, but when we get too much of it, we wear rubbers."

*If a cookie falls on the floor and you pick it up, that's a squat, right? 

A precious little girl walks into a pet shop and asks, with the sweetest little lisp you can imagine, between two missing teeth, "Excuthe me, thir, do you have any widdle wabbits?"

The shopkeeper's heart is melted by this delightful young girl and he gets down on one knee to speak to her properly. "Do you want a widdle white wabbit, or a thoft and fuwwy bwack wabbit, or perhapth one like that cute widdle bwown wabbit over there?"

She looks across at the choice, blushes shyly, rocks on her heels, puts her hands on her knees and leans forward before saying in a quiet voice. "I don't think my python will weawwy give a thit."

*After five years of studying, a student rushes into Einstein's office shouting, "Sir! Sir! I finally understand your Theory of Special Relativity!" Einstein rolls his eyes and says, "It's about time".

A captain in the foreign legion was transferred to a desert outpost. On his orientation tour he noticed a very old, seedy looking camel tied out back of the enlisted men's barracks. He asked the sergeant leading the tour, "What's the camel for?"

The sergeant replied, "Well sir it's a long way from anywhere, and the men have natural sexual urges, so when they do, uh, we have the camel."

The captain said, "Well if it's good for morale, then I guess it's all right with me."

After he had been at the fort for about six months the captain could not stand it anymore so he told his sergeant, "BRING IN THE CAMEL!"

The sergeant shrugged his shoulders and led the camel into the captain's quarters. The captain got a footstool and proceeded to have vigorous sex with the camel. As he stepped down from the stool and buttoned his pants he asked the sergeant, "Is that how the enlisted men do it?"

The sergeant replied, "Well sir, they usually just use it to ride to town and pick up women."

"I have good and bad news," the doctor said to his patient.

"Give me the good news first," the patient said.

"Your test results are back," the doctor said, "and you have only two days to live."

"That's the good news?" the patient exclaimed. "What's the bad news?"

"I've been trying to reach you for two days."

Two hunters are in the woods when one of them collapses. His hunting buddy immediately calls 911.

"My friend isn't breathing," he shouts into the phone. "What should I do?"

"Relax," the operator tells him. "I can help. First, let's make sure he's dead."

There's silence, and then a gunshot. The guy gets back on the phone and says, "OK, now what?"

After a party night in the pub, two Irishmen wake up in a graveyard.

Paddy starts reading the gravestones. "Mick," he says, "would you look at this, a feller here who was 90 when he died!"

"Who's that?" says Mick.

"Somebody called O'Toole from Kerry," Paddy replies.

Mick says, "Never mind him, there's a feller here called Murphy, was 99 when he died! From Castletown of all places!"

"Well that's nothing!" says Paddy. "What about what's written on this feller's stone, here right outside the gate at the edge of the road? The stone says 147!"

"147? That's amazing!" says Mick. "Who was he?"

"Well according to the stone, it's somebody called Miles from Dublin."

A redneck's father passed away in his sleep. So in the morning, he calls 911 to come pick up the body. The 911 operator told him that she would send someone out right away.

"Where do you live?" asked the operator.

He replied, "At the end of Eucalyptus Drive."

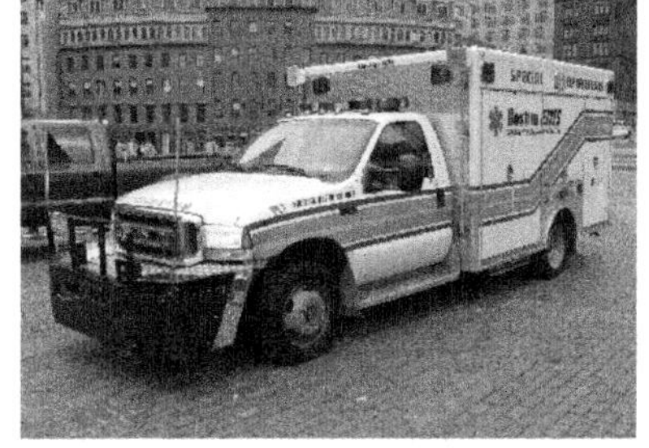

The operator asked, "Can you spell that for me?

There was a long pause and finally he said, "How 'bout if I drag him over to Oak Street and you pick him up there?"

A man is walking through the woods when he sees a bear charging at him.

He books it, but he knows he can't outrun a bear for long, so he starts praying, "Dear Lord, I beseech thee. Please, Lord, please let this bear be a Christian!"

The bear catches up to him, knocks him down on the ground, then gets on its knees and says, "Dear Lord, thank you for this food I am about to receive."

I recently spent $6,500 on a young registered bull. I put him out with the herd, but he just ate grass and wouldn't even look at a cow. I was beginning to think I had paid more for that bull than he was worth.

So I had the vet look at him. He said the bull was very healthy, but possibly just a little young, so he gave me some pills to feed him once per day.

The bull started to service the cows within two days, all my cows! He even broke through the fence and bred my neighbor's cows! He's like a machine!

I don't know what was in the pills the vet gave him but they taste like peppermint.

If you dropped something when you were younger, you just picked it up. When you're older and you drop something, you stare at it for a bit and contemplate whether you actually still need it anymore.

Tim decided to tie the knot with his long-time girlfriend. One evening, after the honeymoon, he was organizing his golfing equipment.

His wife was standing nearby watching him. After a long period of silence she finally speaks: "Tim, I've been thinking, now that we're married maybe it's time you quit golfing. You spend so much time on the course. You could probably get a good price for your clubs."

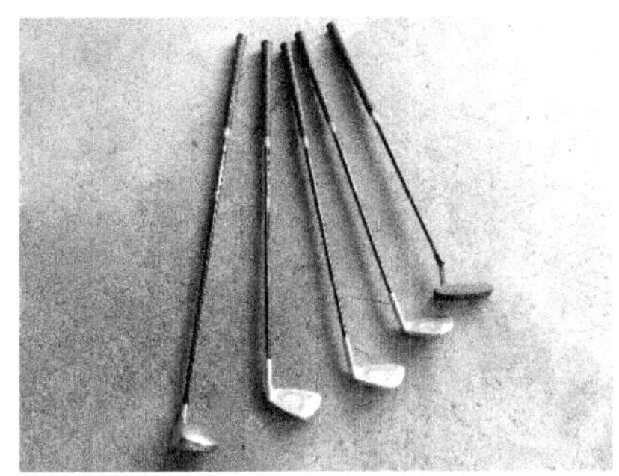

Tim gets this horrified look on his face.

She says, "Darling, what's wrong?"

"For a minute there you were beginning to sound like my ex-wife."

"Ex-wife!" she screams, "I didn't know you were married before!"

"I wasn't," he replied.

Two rednecks are hunting and come upon a huge hole in the ground. They're amazed by the size of it.

The first hunter says, "Wow, that's some hole. I can't even see the bottom. I wonder how deep it is."

The second hunter says, "Let's throw something down and listen, see how long it takes to hit bottom."

The first says, "There's an old engine block over there, give me a hand and we'll throw it in and see."

So they pick it up, carry it over, and throw it in the hole. They're standing, listening and looking over the edge when they hear a rustling in the brush behind them. A goat crashes through the brush and with no hesitation jumps in. While they're gazing into the hole, trying to figure out what that was all about, an old farmer trots up.

"Say there", he says. "You fellers didn't happen to see my goat around here anywhere, did you?"

The first hunter says, "Well, a minute ago a goat came running out of the bushes doin' a hunert miles an hour. It jumped headfirst into this hole here!"

The old farmer said, "Impossible. I had him chained to an old engine block!"

Four older men are walking down a street. They turn a corner and see a sign that says, "Old Timers Bar - ALL drinks 10 cents."They look at each other and then go in, thinking this is too good to be true.

The bartender says in a voice that carries across the room, "Come on in and let me pour one for you! What'll it be, gentlemen? "There's a fully stocked bar, so each of the men orders a martini.
The bartender serves up four iced martinis shaken, not stirred, and says, "That's 10 cents each, please."

The four guys stare at the bartender for a moment, then at each other. They can't believe their good luck. They pay the 40 cents, finish their martinis, and order another round. Again, four excellent martinis are produced, with the bartender again saying, "That's 40 cents, please."

They pay 40 cents, but their curiosity gets the better of them. They've each had two martinis and haven't even spent a dollar yet. Finally, one of them says, "How can you afford to serve martinis as good as these for a dime apiece?"

"I'm a retired tailor from Phoenix," the bartender says, "and I always wanted to own a bar. Last year I hit the Lottery Jackpot for $125 million and decided to open this place. Every drink costs a dime. Wine, liquor, beer—it's all the same."

"Wow! That's some story!" one of the men says.

As the four of them sip their martinis, they can't help noticing seven other people at the end of the bar who don't have any drinks in front of them and haven't ordered anything the whole time they've been there. Nodding at the seven at the end of the bar, one of the men asks the bartender, "What's with them?"

The bartender says, "They're retired people from The Villages, Florida. They're waiting for Happy Hour when drinks are half-price."

*Prayer for Good Health for Seniors:
God grant me the senility to forget the people I never liked anyway, the good fortune to run into the ones I do, and the eyesight to tell the difference.

The wife and I took a long country drive and pulled over to fill up our car's gas tank and tires. She was surprised to see that the station had 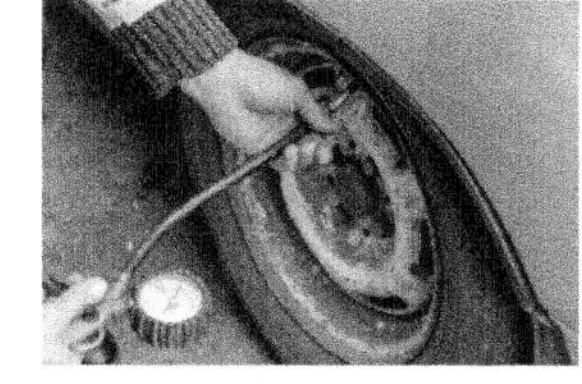 a fee to fill the tires and asked me, "Why in the world do they charge for AIR?!"
I said flatly, "Inflation."

Anyone remember the good old days before Facebook and Instagram when you had to pull out your camera, take a photo of your dinner, then get the  film developed, then go around to your friends' houses to show them the pictures of your dinner? No? Me neither. Stop it.

I got two tickets to the Masters. The person who got them for me didn't realize it was the same day as my wedding. If you're interested, I'm looking for someone to take my place. It's at St. Timothy's in The Villages, Florida at 3 pm. The bride's name is Georgina, she's 5'5" and 125 pounds, and a good cook. She'll be the one in the white dress.

One Sunday the pastor found a pink envelope containing $1,000 in the collection plate. It happened again the next week. The following Sunday, he watched the offering closely and saw a little old lady drop another pink envelope in the plate. After weeks of this, the pastor approached her.

"Ma'am, I couldn't help but notice that you put $1,000 a week in the collection plate," he said.

"Every week my son sends $10,000, so I share it with the church," she admitted.

"Wow. He must be very successful," the pastor said.

"He is a veterinarian," she answered.

"That's an honorable profession, pastor said. "Where does he practice?"

"In Nevada," the old lady said proudly, "He has two cat houses, one in Las Vegas and one in Reno."

A climber falls off a cliff. As he tumbles down he catches hold of a small branch. It's hundreds of feet to the bottom. "Help!" he shouts. "Is there anybody up there?"

A voice booms through the gorge, "I will help you, my son, but first you must have faith in me."

"Yes, yes, I trust you!" cries the man.

"Let go of the branch," commands the voice.

There's a long pause, and the man shouts up again, "Is there anybody else up there?"

*Me (sobbing my heart out, eyes swollen, nose red): "I can't see you anymore. I'm not going to let you hurt me like this again!"

Trainer "It was a sit-up. You did one sit-up."

A nun walks into Mother Superior's office and lets out a heavy sigh. "What troubles you, Sister?' asked Mother Superior. "Wasn't this the day you spent with your family?"

"It was," said the Sister. "And I went to play golf with my brother. You know I was quite a talented golfer before I devoted my life to Christ."

"I recall that," Mother said. "So it wasn't relaxing?"

"No, plus, I took the Lord's name in vain today!"

"Goodness, Sister! Tell me about it."

"Well, we were on the fifth tee. The hole is a monster, 540 yards, Par 5, nasty dogleg left, hidden green. I hit the drive of my life. Sweetest swing I ever made. And it's flying straight and true, right along the line I wanted—and it hits a bird in midflight!"

"Oh no!' commiserated the Mother. "That so unlucky. But surely that didn't make you blaspheme, Sister!"

"Not that, no. I'm standing there shocked, and this squirrel runs out of the woods, grabs my ball and runs off down the fairway!"

"Oh, that would have made me blaspheme!" exclaimed the Mother Superior.

"But I didn't!" sobbed the Sister. "I held back. But then this hawk swoops down and grabs the squirrel and flies off, with my ball still clutched in his paws!"

"So that's when you cursed," said the Mother.

"Nope, that wasn't it either," cried the Sister, "because as the hawk started to fly away, the squirrel struggled and the hawk dropped him onto the green. The ball popped out of his paws and rolled to about 18 inches from the cup!"

Mother Superior sat back in her chair, folded her arms across her chest, fixed the Sister with a baleful stare and said, "You missed the effin putt, didn't you?"

Two campers are walking through the woods when a huge brown bear suddenly appears in the clearing about 50 feet in front of them. The bear sees the campers and begins to head toward them.

The first guy drops his backpack, digs out a pair of sneakers, and frantically begins to put them on.

The second guy says, "What are you doing? Sneakers won't help you outrun that bear."

"I don't need to outrun the bear," the first guy says. "I just need to outrun you."

I was in my garden when I got the news that my father had fallen from a 20-foot ladder and was in the hospital. I rushed to the hospital expecting that my father had some major fractures, but he was alright except for some minor cuts. When I told him that it was a miracle, he disagreed and told me, "Son, I only fell from the first step of the ladder."

A woman told her friend, "I feel like my body has gotten totally out of shape, so I got my doctor's permission to join a fitness club and start exercising. I decided to take an aerobics class for seniors. I bent, twisted, gyrated, jumped up and down, and perspired for an hour. But by the time I got my leotards on, the class was already over."

A patrol cop called the police dispatcher on his radio. "I have an interesting case here. An old lady shot her husband for stepping on the floor she just mopped."
"Have you arrested the woman?" asked the dispatcher.
"Not yet. The floor's still wet."

Boy "Wow, so many scars. You must have had an adventurous life!"
Old man: "No, I just have a cat."

A Muslim couple, preparing to wed, meet the Mullah for counseling. He asks if they have questions.

The man says, "It is Islam tradition for men to dance with men, women to dance with women. At our reception, we'd like permission to dance together."

"Absolutely not," says the Mullah. "It's immoral. Men and women always dance separately."

"So, after the ceremony, I can't even dance with my own wife?"

"No," answers the Mullah, "It's forbidden in Islam."

"Well, okay," says the man, "What about sex? Can we finally have sex?"

"Of course!" replies the Mullah, "Sex is OK within marriage, to have children!"

"What about different positions?" asks the man.

"No problem," says the Mullah.

"Woman on top? Woman below?"

"Sure," says the Mullah, go for it!"

"On the kitchen table?"

"Yes, yes!"

"Can we do it with all my four wives together on rubber sheets with a bottle of hot oil, a couple of vibrators, leather harnesses, a bucket of honey, a camel and a goat?"

"You may indeed!"

"Can we do it standing up?"

"No." says the Mullah."

"Why not?" asks the man.

"It could lead to dancing."

A Husband and Wife at Custody court. The judge looks sternly at the ex-wife.

Judge: "Why do you think you deserve custody of the child?"

Ex-wife: "I brought him into this world so I should have custody of him."

Judge: "That is a simple yet good reason."

The judge looks towards the ex-husband and asks, "Why do you think you deserve custody of the child?

The ex-husband thought long and hard about his response, after a brief moment of silence, he replies, "If I put money into a Pepsi machine and a Pepsi comes out, is it mine or is it the machine's?"

*I told my physical therapist I broke my arm in two places. He told me to stop going to those places.

As a group of robbers entered the bank, their leader went to the manager and told him to open the vault, saying, "If you try to do anything smart, you're fiction.'" 

The manager asked, "Don't you mean, 'You're history?"

The robber angrily replied, "Don't change the subject."

A man and his wife are at a restaurant, and the husband keeps staring at an old drunken lady swigging her gin.

His wife asks, "Do you know her?"

"Yes," sighs the husband. "She's my ex-wife. She took to drinking right after we divorced seven years ago, and I hear she hasn't been sober since."

"My God!" says the wife. "Who would think a person could go on celebrating that long?"

A boy read a restaurant sign that advertised fat-free French fries.

"Sounds great," said the health-conscious boy. He ordered some. He watched as the cook pulled a basket of fries from the fryer. The potatoes were dripping with oil when the cook put them into the container.

"Wait a minute," the boy said. "Those don't look fat-free." 

"Sure they are," the cook said. "We charge only for the potatoes."

*After a big fight, my wife yelled at me, "You know, I was a fool when I married you." So I replied, "That may be true, but I was in love and didn't notice that."

*Money isn't everything, but it sure keeps you in touch with your children.

A farmer is selling his prize-winning bull. A woman buys it for $5000.

A week later he learns that the bull has died, so he calls the woman and offers to give her back her money, but she says no. She explains, "I held a raffle. $100 a ticket for the bull. Five hundred people bought in, which is $50,000."

The farmer asks if people were upset because the bull died.

"Not at all. Only the winner, so I refunded his $100 ticket."

*If I ever decide to buy a horse ranch in my old age, I'm going to name it "Pasture Prime."

*What's the secret to having a smoking hot body as a senior? Cremation.

*"I'm at an age when my back goes out more than I do."

*Now that I've gotten older, everything's finally starting to click for me. My knees, my back, my neck.

An older gentleman shuffled slowly into an ice cream parlor and pulled himself slowly, rather painfully, onto a stool. After catching his breath, he ordered a banana split supreme. The waitress smiled kindly at him, asking "crushed nuts?"

 The older gentleman replied, "No. Arthritis."

*You know you're old when getting lucky means a short wait in the doctor's office.

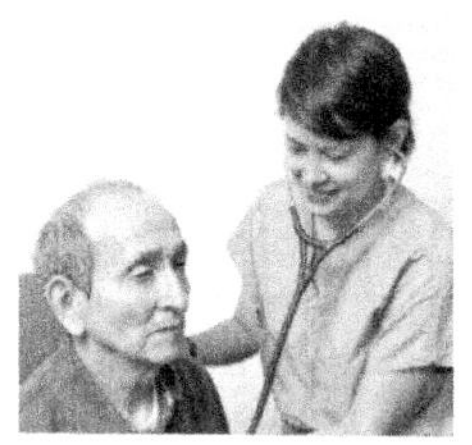

An older man decided to add a pet companion to his life, so he buys a parrot and brings it home. However, the parrot almost immediately starts insulting him and gets really rude. In a moment of frustration, the man picks up the parrot and tosses it into the freezer to teach it a lesson. But when the bird stops squawking, the man panics and opens the freezer.

The parrot walks out, looks up at the man, and says, "I apologize for offending you, and I humbly ask your forgiveness." 

The man says, "I forgive you, and I'm sorry too."

The parrot then says, "If you don't mind my asking… what'd the turkey do?"

I went to see my dentist and he warned me it was going to hurt. He ended up telling me he was having an affair with my wife. 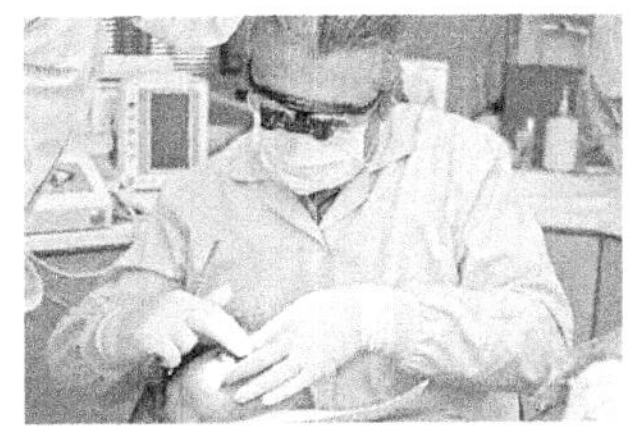

Sven walks up to a three-holer outhouse and finds his neighbor Ole fishing around in the hole with a long stick. Sven asks Ole what he's doing.

"Vell, I sat down dere to go and when I set my barn coat to the side, da darn coat slipped into de odder hole. I need to get it." 

Sven says, "Ole, are you cuckoo in da head? You don't wanna wear dat coat after it's been down dere.

"No vay, Sven. I am not a stupid man. But in de pocket dere's two lutefisk sammiches."

*My wife left a note on the fridge: "This isn't working." I opened the fridge door; it works fine. 

My wife of 60 years told me, "Let's go upstairs and make love."
I said, "Choose one."

A couple's mischievous boys kept getting into trouble. The parents heard a clergyman in town had been successful in disciplining children, so she asked if he'd speak with her boys. He agreed and asked to see them individually. So the mother sent her 8-year-old in the morning, the older boy in the afternoon.

The clergyman sat the younger boy down and asked him sternly, "Where is God?" The boy sat with his mouth hanging open, wide-eyed. So the clergyman repeated the question in an even sterner tone, "Where is God!!?" Again the boy made no attempt to answer. The clergyman raised his voice, shook his finger in the boy's face and bellowed, "WHERE IS GOD!?"

The boy screamed and bolted from the room, ran directly home and hid on the back porch. When his older brother found him, he asked, "What happened?" 

The younger brother, gasping for breath, replied, "We are in BIG trouble this time, dude. God is missing and they think WE did it!"

It was Friday entertainment night at the seniors' home. It was a special night and all one hundred and fifty residents were in attendance.

After the community sing-along led by Alice at the piano, it was time for the star of the show. Claude the Hypnotist who'd come all the way from Montreal!

Claude explained that he was going to put the whole audience into a trance. "Yes, each and every one of you, all at the same time," he said.

The excited chatter dropped to silence as Claude carefully withdrew, from his waistcoat pocket, a beautiful antique gold pocket watch and chain.

"I want you to keep your eyes on this watch," said Claude, holding the watch for all to see. "It's a very special watch made by a renowned watchmaker in Paris and has been in my family for six generations."

He began to swing the watch gently back and forth while quietly chanting, "Watch the watch, watch the watch, watch the watch."

The audience was mesmerized as the watch swayed back and forth. The lights reflected off the watch's gleaming surface. A hundred and fifty pairs of eyes followed the movements of the gently swaying watch. They were all hypnotized.

And then, suddenly, the chain broke! The beautiful watch fell to the floor and burst apart on impact.

"S&!T," shouted Claude.

They did. All 150 residents had bowel movements in unison. It took them three days to completely clean up the lounge and Claude was never invited back again.

*As I get older, I remember all the people I lost along the way. Maybe a career as a tour guide was not the right choice.

Jock had been a religious man all his life. When rushed into hospital his family called a preacher to stand with them. As the preacher stood next to the bed, Jock's condition appeared to worsen and he motioned frantically for something to write on. He was lovingly handed a pen and paper and Jock used his last gasp to scribble a note which he handed to the preacher and then he died.

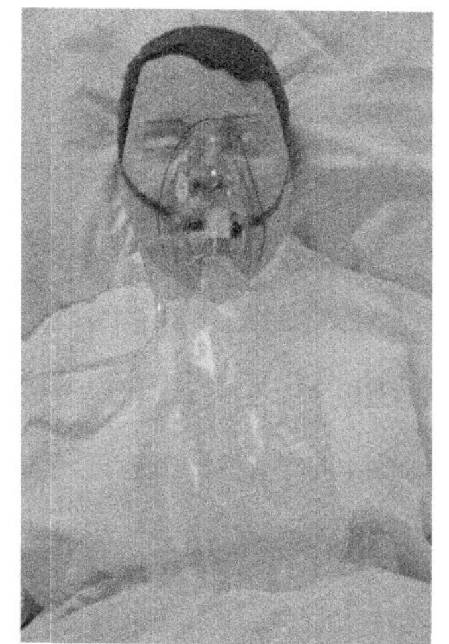

The preacher thought it best not to look at the note at the time and placed it in his jacket pocket.

At the funeral, as he was finishing his eulogy he realized that he was wearing the same jacket as he had at the hospital. He said "You know, Auld Jock handed me a wee note just before he died. I haven't read it yet, but knowing Auld Jock I'm sure there's a word of inspiration there for us all"

He opened the note and read out loud "Hi minister. Yer standin on ma oxygen."

It's the middle of winter and a primary school teacher was helping one of her pupils put on his boots at the end of the day. The boy asked for help and she could see why. Even with her pulling and him pushing, the little boots still didn't want to go on. By the time they got the second boot on, she had worked up a sweat. He then announced, "These aren't my boots".

She bit her tongue and resisted the temptation to say, "Why didn't you say so?" Once again, she struggled to help him pull the ill-fitting boots off his little feet.

No sooner had they got the boots off when he said, "They're my brother's boots. But my mum made me wear 'em today".

Now she didn't know if she should laugh or cry. But she mustered up what grace and courage she had left to wrestle the boots back onto his feet again. Helping him into his coat, she asked, "Now, where are your mittens?"

He said, "I stuffed 'em in the toes of my boots".

A farmer needed to buy a rooster for his chickens. Another man had a rooster for sale. The farmer goes to buy the rooster, and the man tells him this is Brewster, he will service your chickens, but he is a sex addict and will go after anything.

The farmer buys Brewster and takes him home. Brewster goes through the henhouse, then starts on the farmer's sheep and other barnyard animals. After a couple days of this, the farmer tells Brewster, "You gotta slow down or you'll kill yourself."
After a week of Brewster going after every animal on the farm, the farmer comes out and sees Brewster laid out in the yard, ten vultures already waiting in the tree nearby. The farmer, cussing, tells the corpse of his rooster, "I told you you'd kill yourself if you didn't stop your sex-crazed ways."
Brewster opens one eye and says, "Shut up, they're about to land."

Days before Christmas a mom calls her daughter and says, "Hey, I know it's a shock, but I'm pregnant."

"How could this happen?" the shocked daughter says. "You're forty-six, Mom. This is unbelievable"

"It was an accident. Just call your sister and tell her."

The daughter frantically calls her sister who then calls their mom. "Mom, I don't understand," she says. "The two of us are flying home right away. I'm booking the flights now." She hangs up the phone.

The mom pops the cork on a bottle of champagne, pours a glass for herself and one for her husband. "Told you I could do it. The girls are coming home for Christmas and they're paying for their own plane tickets."

I blame my mother for my poor life in the bedroom. All she told me was, 'The man goes on top and the woman underneath.' For three years my husband and I slept in bunk beds. –Joan Rivers

Tiger Woods & Stevie Wonder are in a bar. Tiger says to Stevie, "How's the singing career going?"

Stevie replies, "Not too bad. How's the golf?"

Woods replies, "Not too bad, I've had some problems with my swing, but I think I've got that right, now."

Stevie: "I always find that when my swing goes wrong, I need to stop playing for a while and not think about it. Next time it seems to be all right."

Incredulous, Tiger says, "You play GOLF?"

Stevie: "Yes, I've been playing for years."

Tiger: "But you're blind! How can you play golf?"

Stevie: "Well, I get my caddy to stand in the middle of the fairway and call to me. I listen for the sound of his voice and play the ball towards him. Then, when I get to where the ball lands the caddy moves to the green or farther down the fairway and again I play the ball towards his voice."

"But how do you putt?" asks Tiger.

"Well", says Stevie, "I get my caddy to lean down in front of the hole and call to me with his head on the ground and I just play the ball towards his voice."

Tiger: "What's your handicap?"

Stevie: "Well, actually I'm a scratch golfer."

Woods, incredulous, says to Stevie, "We've got to play a round sometime."

Stevie: "Well, people don't take me seriously, so I only play for money, and never play for less than $10,000 a hole. Is that a problem?"

Woods thinks about it and says, "I can afford that OK, I'm game for that. And $10,000 a hole is fine with me. When would you like to play?"

Stevie: "Pick a night."

A young woman in New York decided to end her life by throwing herself into the ocean. She went down to the docks and was about to leap into the frigid water when a handsome young sailor saw her tottering on the edge of the pier, crying.

He took pity and said, "Look, you have so much to live for. I'm off to Europe in the morning, and if you like, I can stow you away on my ship. I'll take good care of you and bring you food every day."

Moving closer, he slipped his arm around her shoulder and added, "I'll keep you happy, and you'll keep me happy."

The girl nodded yes. After all, what did she have to lose? Perhaps a fresh start in Europe would give her life new meaning.

That night, the sailor brought her aboard and hid her in a lifeboat. From then on, every night he brought her three sandwiches and a piece of fruit, and they made passionate love until dawn.

Three weeks later, during a routine inspection, she was discovered by the captain.

"What are you doing here?" the captain asked.

"I have an arrangement with one of the sailors," she explained. "I get food and a trip to Europe, and he's screwing me."

"He certainly is," the captain said. "This is the Staten Island ferry."

When ordering food at a restaurant, I asked the waiter, "How do you prepare the chicken?"

"Nothing special," he explained. "We just tell it it's going to die."

"Dear," asked the wife. "What would you do if I died?"

"Why, dear, I would be extremely upset," answered the husband. "Why do you ask?"

"Would you remarry?" persevered the wife.

"No, of course not, love," replied the husband.

"Do you like being married?" asked the wife.

"Of course I do, lamb." he said.

"Then why wouldn't you remarry?"

"All right," said the husband, taking a different tack to end the conversation. "I'd remarry, then."

"You would?" responded the wife, looking pained.

"Yes," replied the trapped husband.

"Would you sleep with her in OUR bed?" asked the wife after a very long pause.

"Well, I suppose," said the tiring mate.

"I see," said the wife quite sternly and indignantly.

"And would you let her wear my old clothes?"

"I suppose, if she wanted to," stammered her mate, adding, "it would be a compliment to your exquisite taste."

"Really," replied the wife icily. "And would you take down the pictures of me and replace them with pictures of her?"

"I don't know. But wouldn't that be the correct thing to do?" he replied.

"Is that so?" said the wife, leaping to her feet. "And I suppose you'd let her play with my golf clubs, too."

"Of course not, dear. That would be impossible. She's left-handed."

A retired man drove his brand-new Mercedes to 100 mph. In his rearview mirror he saw a police car, so he sped up to 120 then 140. When he could see he couldn't outrun the cruiser, he pulled over.

The officer walked up, looked at his watch and said, "Sir, my shift ends in ten minutes. Today is Friday and I'm taking off for the weekend with my family. If you can give me a good reason I've never heard before why you were speeding, I'll let you go."

The man looked seriously at the cop and answered, "Years ago, my wife ran off with a policeman. I was afraid you were bringing her back."

The cop said, "Have a good day," and walked away.

*A study has found that women who carry a little extra weight live longer than the men who mention it.

*The doctor gave me a year to live, so I shot him. The judge gave me 15 years. Problem solved.

A couple were celebrating their golden wedding anniversary. Their domestic tranquility had long been the talk of the town. A local newspaper reporter was inquiring as to the secret of their long and happy marriage.

"Well, it dates back to our honeymoon," explained the man. "We visited the Grand Canyon and took a trip down to the bottom of the canyon by pack mule. We hadn't gone too far when my wife's mule stumbled. My wife quietly said, 'That's once.' We proceeded a little further and the mule stumbled again. My wife quietly said, 'That's twice.' Hadn't gone a half- mile when the mule stumbled the third time. My wife quietly removed a revolver from her pocket and shot the mule dead. I started to yell at her for her treatment of the mule when she looked at me and whispered, 'That's once.'"

*I thought I married Mister Right.
Turns out his first name is Always.

A crusty old sergeant major found himself at a gala event, hosted by a local liberal arts college. There was no shortage of extremely young, idealistic ladies in attendance, one of whom approached the sergeant major for conversation.

She said, "Excuse me, sergeant major, but you seem to be a very serious man. Is something bothering you?"

"Negative, ma'am," the sergeant major said, "Just serious by nature."

The young lady looked at his awards and decorations and said, "It looks like you have seen a lot of action."

The sergeant major's short reply was, "Yes, ma'am, a lot of action."

The young lady, tiring of trying to start up a conversation, said, "You know, you should lighten up a little. Relax and enjoy yourself."

The sergeant major just stared at her in his serious manner.

Finally the young lady said, "You know, I hope you don't take this the wrong way, but when is the last time you had sex?"

The sergeant major looked at her and replied, "1955."

She said, "Well, there you are. You really need to chill out and quit taking everything so seriously! I mean, no sex since 1955! Isn't that a little extreme?"

The sergeant major, glancing at his watch, said in his matter-of-fact voice, "You think so? It's only 2130 now."

A woman goes to the dentist and the dentist tells her she needs a root canal.'

She says, "A root canal? Crap! I'd rather have another baby than a root canal!"

He says, "Make up your mind. I gotta adjust the chair."

*A shipment of Viagra was stolen yesterday by a gang of old men. Police are now on the lookout for these hardened criminals.

A farmer stopped by the local mechanics shop to have his truck fixed. They couldn't do it while he waited, so he said he'd just walk the mile home.

On the way he stopped at the hardware store for a bucket and a gallon of paint. He then stopped by the feed store and picked up a couple of chickens and a goose. However, struggling outside the store he now had a problem carrying his purchases home.

While he was scratching his head, he was approached by a little old lady who said she was lost. "Can you tell me how to get to 1603 Mockingbird Lane?"

The farmer said, "Matter of fact, my farm is close to there. I'd walk you there but I can't carry this lot."

The old lady suggested, "Why don't you put the can of paint in the bucket, carry the bucket in one hand, put a chicken under each arm, and carry the goose in your other hand?"

"Why thank you very much," he said and they started walking. On the way he says, "Let's take my shortcut and go down this alley. We'll be there in no time."

The little old lady looked him cautiously then said, "I am a lonely widow without a husband to defend me. How do I know that when we get in the alley you won't hold me up against the wall, pull up my skirt, and have your way with me?"

The farmer said, "Holy smokes lady! I'm carrying a bucket, a gallon of paint, two chickens, and a goose. How in the world could I possibly hold you up against the wall and do that?"

The old lady replied, "Set the goose down, cover him with the bucket, put the paint on top of the bucket, and I'll hold the chickens."

*Marriage is like a deck of cards. All you need at first is two hearts and a diamond. But by the end you wish you had a club and a spade.

*You don't need a parachute to skydive, but you need a parachute to skydive twice.

A televangelist, a rabbi, and a Hindu holy man had car trouble and asked to spend the night with a farmer. He said, "I only have room for two inside, so one of you must sleep in the barn."

"No problem," said the rabbi. "My people wandered in the desert for forty years, I am humble enough to sleep in the barn for an evening." So he departed to the barn as the others bedded down inside.

Moments later came a knock and the farmer opened the door to find the rabbi. "What's wrong?" asked the farmer. The rabbi said, "There is a pig in the barn and my faith believes a pig is an unclean animal." His Hindu friend agrees to swap places. A few minutes there's a knock on the door. The farmer opens it. The Hindu says, "I am grateful but there is a cow in the barn. In my country cows are sacred. I can't sleep on holy ground!"

That leaves only the televangelist. He grumbled and complained, but went to the barn. Moments later came another knock on the farmer's door. Frustrated and tired, the farmer opens the door to find the pig and the cow.

A woman was driving home from Northern Arizona when she saw an elderly Navajo woman walking along the road. After considering the distance she still had to drive and not wanting to do it in silence, she stopped and asked the older adult if she'd like a ride. The latter showed her appreciation and got in the car.

As the journey continued, the elderly Navaho noticed the driver's brown bag and got curious. She asked what was in the bag, and the younger adult said, "It's a bottle of wine. Got it for my husband."

The Navajo woman went silent for a bit then replied with an aura of wisdom in her voice, "Good trade."

Two nuns snuck out to the local tavern and got smashed. When they got back to the convent, they tried to climb over the wrought iron fence. As one nun helped the second get over, the second said, "I feel like a Marine!"

The first nun replied "So do I, but where will we find one at this time of night?"

In a trial a Southern small-town prosecuting attorney called his first witness, a grandmotherly, elderly woman to the stand. He approached her and asked, "Mrs. Jones, do you know me?"

She responded, "Why, yes, I do know you, Mr. Williams. I've known you since you were a boy, and frankly, you've been a big disappointment to me. You lie, you cheat on your wife, and you manipulate people and talk about them behind their backs. You think you're a big shot when you haven't the brains to realize you'll never amount to anything more than a two-bit paper pusher. Yes, I know you."

The lawyer was stunned. Not knowing what else to do, he pointed across the room and asked, "Mrs. Jones, do you know the defense attorney?"

She again replied, "Why yes, I do. I've known Mr. Bradley since he was a youngster, too. He's lazy, bigoted, and he has a drinking problem. He can't build a normal relationship with anyone, and his law practice is one of the worst in the entire state. Not to mention he cheated on his wife with three different women. One was your wife. Yes, I know him."

The defense attorney nearly died.

The judge asked both counselors to approach the bench and, in a very quiet voice, said, "If either of you idiots asks her if she knows me, I'll send you both to the electric chair!"

Bob, a golfer, is just about to take his shot at the tenth hole when he sees a funeral cortege driving down the

road adjacent to the course. He stands to attention, removes his hat and bows his head.

His friend says, "Well that's a surprise Bob, I've never seen you so well behaved and respectable."

Bob replies, "Well it's the least I can do. I've been married to her for thirty years."

Ole hadn't been feeling too well, so he went to see his doctor. A week later the doctor called Ole and told him to come in so he could go over the test results with him, and be sure to bring his wife, Lena.

"Ole, I don't know any gentle way to tell you this, so I'm going to be blunt. You have an incurable disease, and there's nothing we can do to help you. Set your affairs in order, because you only have about two weeks to live."

Ole was very quiet for a moment, and then turned to his wife, Lena. "Lena, I vant you to promise me sumting. I vant you to promise me dat after I'm gone, you'll marry Lars Larson."

"Lars Larson? Ole, you've hated him all your life!" Ole said "Yup. Still do."

Over the next two weeks, Ole got sicker and weaker. One afternoon, he woke up in bed and smelled the delightful aroma of freshly baked chocolate chip cookies wafting through the house. With every bit of strength he had, Ole made his way to the kitchen. He thought to himself, I guess Lena really does love me! She knows how much I love chocolate chip cookies, and she baked some to try to cheer me up! He managed to pour himself a glass of milk, and sat down at the table.

 He had just taken a bite of a cookie when Lena came in. "Ole! Vat you doing? You should be in bed, not out here eating cookies! Doze are for da funeral!"

Well, Ole died. Lena went down to the local newspaper to have the death notice printed. The printer asked her what she wanted it to say. "Yust print 'Ole died.'"

"That's all?" asked the printer.

"Yep, dat's all."

"Well, you know, Lena, the first 5 words are free."

Lena thought for a moment. "OK, den print dis: 'Ole died. Boat for sale.'"

A couple in their 70s visited a sex therapist. The therapist said he needed to observe them, and asked if they'd be okay with him watching them through a one-way mirror. They agreed. Afterward, the therapist said everything was normal and that they were doing great considering their age. The couple were happy to hear that and left after paying the man's $50 co-pay. Surprisingly, the couple returned every Wednesday for six weeks, repeating the routine. The confused therapist asked why.

The man explained, "Well, we can't do it at my place because my wife is there, and we can't do it at her place because her husband is there.
The least expensive hotels charge $130 a night. But my co-pay here is only $50. Do the math." 

Beer bottle: break me and you get year of bad luck.

Mirror: Break me and you get 7 years of bad luck.

Condom: walks off laughing

Ole and Sven went fishing one day in a rented boat and were catching fish like crazy. Ole said, "We better mark dis spot so ve can come back tomorrow and catch more fish."

When Sven marked the bottom of the boat with a large X, Ole asked him what he was doing.

"Marking the spot so tomorrow we can catch more fish."

Ole said, "Ya big dummy, how do ya know ve'll get da same boat tomorrow?"

At the marriage retreat, the instructor talked about the importance of knowing what matters to each other.

"For example," he began, pointing to Ole. "Do you know your wife's favorite flower?"

Ole answered, "You betcha. Pillsbury All Purpose."

A nun walked into a local Hooters. The place was hopping with music and loud conversation and every once in a 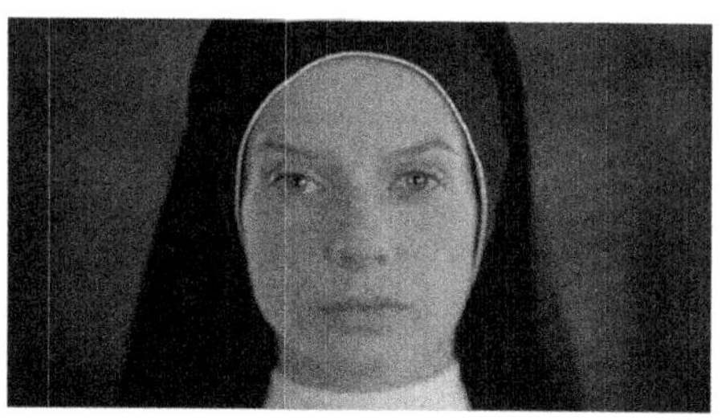 while, the lights would turn off and the place would erupt into cheers. But when the revelers saw the nun, the room went dead silent, which didn't surprise her. She asked the bartender where the restroom was.

The bartender pointed down a hallway and said, "I should warn you, Sister, there's a statue of a naked man in there wearing only a fig leaf."

"I can just look the other way," said the nun, and started for the hallway at a brisk pace. "I really have to go."

After a few minutes she came back out and the whole place stopped its revelry long enough to give her a loud round of applause.

She said to the bartender, "Why did they applaud for me just because I went to the restroom?"

"Well, now they know you're one of us. Would you like a free drink?"

"No thank you, I don't drink. And I still don't understand," said the puzzled nun.

"You see," laughed the bartender, "every time someone lifts the fig leaf on that statue, the lights go out." He winked, and said, "Now how about that drink?"

A man arrives at the bar, seemingly upset. He orders an expensive liquor shot and downs it right away.

He says, "One more!" and the bartender puts one up. The man downs it and says, "One more!" After five shots, the man confesses, "If you had what I have, you'd be drinking this fast too."

Sympathetic, the bartender asks, "Whatcha got?"

The man says, "Less than two dollars."

My new primary care doctor said, "You're
doing fairly well for your age."

So I asked, "Do you think I'll live to be 80?"

The doc asked, "Do you smoke tobacco or drink beer
or wine? Use drugs? Eat red meat and barbecued
ribs? Do you spend a lot of time in the sun, like
playing golf, sailing, hiking, or bicycling? Do you
gamble, drive fast cars, or have a lot of sex?"

"No," I said. "I don't do any of those things."

Doc replied, "So why do you want to live to be 80?"

A priest and a blonde nun are in a car at a stop light
in Transylvania when a vampire blocks their car. The
priest is driving and tells the blonde nun, "Quick,
Sister, show him your cross!"
She rolls down her window and yells, "Get you fat
butt out of the road, you stupid jackass vampire!"

A preacher visits an elderly woman from his congregation. As he sits on the couch, he notices a large bowl of peanuts on the coffee table.

"Mind if I have a few?" he asks.

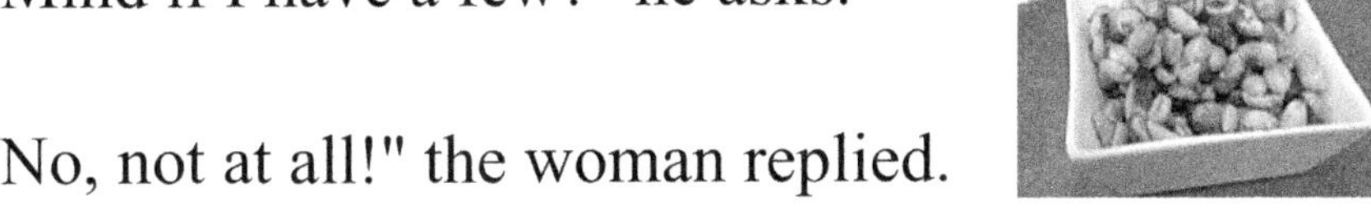

"No, not at all!" the woman replied.

They chat for an hour and, as the preacher stands to leave, he realizes that instead of eating just a few peanuts, he emptied most of the bowl.

"I'm terribly sorry for eating all your peanuts. I really just meant to eat a few."

"Oh, that's all right," the woman says. "Ever since I lost my teeth, all I can do is suck the chocolate off them."

*The worst time to have a heart attack is during a game of charades.

Senior Citizen Texting Codes

ATD - At The Doctors

BFF - Best Friend Fell

BTW - Bring the Wheelchair

BYOT - Bring Your Own Teeth

FWIW - Forgot Where I Was

GGPBL - Gotta Go, Pacemaker Battery Low

GHA - Got Heartburn Again

IMHAO - Is My Hearing-Aid On

LMDO - Laughing My Dentures Out

OMMR - On My Massage Recliner

OMSG - Oh My! Sorry, Gas

TTYL - Talk to You Louder

ROFLACGU - Rolling on Floor Laughing and Can't Get Up

Did you hear what happened when the guy who wrote the song *The Hokey Pokey* died? They couldn't close his coffin. Every time they put his right foot in, he put his left foot out.

A nun walks into Mother Superior's office.

"Terrible news, Mother Superior. We've discovered a case of syphilis in the convent."

Mother Superior looks up, "Wonderful. I was getting tired of the Chablis."

*It's important to establish a good vocabulary. If I'd known the difference between the words *antidote* and *anecdote*, one of my best friends would still be alive.

*Wife: I want another baby.
Husband: That's a relief, I really don't like this one.

Mr. Goldstein was at the end of his life in a nursing home. One day he appeared to be very sad and depressed. Nurse Tracy asked if anything was wrong.

He said, "My private part died today, and I am sad."

Knowing her patients were forgetful and sometimes a little crazy, she replied, "Oh, I'm so sorry, Mr. Goldstein, please accept my condolences."

The following day, Mr. Goldstein was walking down the hall with his private part hanging out of his pajamas, when he met Nurse Tracy.

"Mr. Goldstein," she said, "You shouldn't be walking down the hall like that. Please put your private part back inside your pajamas."

"But, Nurse Tracy," replied Mr. Goldstein, "I told you yesterday that my private part died."

"Yes, you did tell me that, but why is it hanging out of your pajamas?" asked Nurse Tracy.

"Well," he replied. "Today's the viewing."

Revisions of 60s and 70s songs for Boomers

Bobby Darin - *Splish Splash, I Was Havin' a Flash*

Herman's Hermits - *Mrs. Brown, You've Got a Lovely Walker*

Beatles - *I Get By With a Little Help from Depends*

Bee Gees - *How Do You Mend a Broken Hip?*

Roberta Flack - *The First Time Ever I Forgot Your Face*

Johnny Nash - *I Can't See Clearly Now*

Paul Simon - *Fifty Ways to Lose Your Liver*

The Commodores - *Once, Twice, Three Times the Bathroom*

Procol Harum - *A Whiter Shade of Hair*

Leo Sayer - *You Make Me Feel Like Napping*

The Temptations - *Papa's Got a Kidney Stone*

ABBA - *Denture Queen*

Tony Orlando - *Knock 3 Times on the Ceiling If You Hear Me Fall*

Helen Reddy - *I Am Woman, Hear Me Snore*

Lesley Gore - *It's My Procedure and I'll Cry If I Want to*

Willie Nelson - *On the Commode Again*

***Dumb Jokes for Adults** (2025)*
***Cornstalkers** (2024)*
***Kite Boy** (2024)*
***Ghost Pets** (2024)*
***Kids on the Case** (2024)*
***Protect the Queen** (2023)*
***Dumb Jokes for Kids #3** (2022)*
***Dumb Jokes for Kids #2** (2022)*
***Dumb Jokes for Kids #1** (2022)*
***Love Is a Four-Legged Word** (2022)*
***New England Seaside, Roadside, Graveside** (2021)*
***New England Christmas Sampler** (2021)*
***The Bookseller's Daughter** (2019)*
***Fourth Worst Joke Book** (2016)*
***Third Worst Joke Book** (2016)*
***Second Worst Joke Book** (2016)*
***First Worst Joke Book** (2016)*
***Christmas Soup for the Soul** (2016)*
***Publish Your Book Free** (2015)*
***Vampires, Ghosts, and Graveyards** (2015)*
***Horrors** (2015)*
***Wicked Strange** (2015)*
***Vermont Ghost Busters** (2015)*
***FreeK Week** (2014)*
***FreeK Show** (2012)*
***FreeK Camp** (2010)*
***Wicked Odd** (2005)*
***Oddest Yet** (2004)*
***Even Odder** (2003)*
***Odd Lot** (2001)*
***A Christmas Dozen** (2001)*
***The Little Church that Could** (2000)*
***Unk's Fiddle** (1995)*
***What Do You Say to a Burning Bush?** (1995)*
***My Lord, He's Loose in the World!** (1994)*
***Raising Small Church Esteem** (1992)*
***Christmas Special Delivery** (1991)*
***Fingerprints on the Chalice** (1990)*
***Activating Leadership in the Small Church** (1988)*
***Can-U?! Car-Top Canoeist Guide** (1976)*

New York Book Festival grand prize
Florida Book Festival grand prize
Bram Stoker Award for Young Readers (2004)
Bram Stoker Nominee/Finalist (2003)
Mom's Choice Awards gold medal
Moonbeam Children's Book Award
Benjamin Franklin Award
New England Book Festival Award
Halloween Book Festival Award
Hollywood Book Festival Award
New York Book Festival Award
London Book Festival Award
Paris Book Festival Award
Beach Book Festival Award
San Francisco Book Festival Award
Writer's Digest Self-Published Book Award
Independent Publisher Book Award
Foreword Book Awards
Ray Bradbury creative writing prize

Printed in Dunstable, United Kingdom